# The Alchemy of Us

*A Journey Through Twin Flames,*

*Sacred Love, and Soul Remembrance*

blanche johanna

© 2025 blanche johanna

All rights reserved.

No part of this publication may be reproduced, stored in a retrieval system, or transmitted in any form or by any means, electronic, mechanical, photocopying, recording, or otherwise, without the prior written permission of the author.

This book is a spiritual and creative transmission intended to support personal and collective awakening. All guidance and reflections are shared from the author's lived and intuitive experience and are not intended as a substitute for professional advice.

The Alchemy of Us™ is a trademark of blanche johanna. All rights reserved.

ISBN: 978-1-7641285-0-6

www.blanchejohanna.com

## **Dedication**

You have been my mirror, my fire, my sanctuary
Through every unraveling and every rising
you revealed the alchemy of love's true form

In your presence, I found pieces of myself I had long forgotten
Through you, I came home, to truth, to wholeness, to the soul I have always been

And to the one within me who never stopped believing
To the woman who chose light when it was easier to turn away
To the soul who remembered, again and again
This is for you, too

You are the love you've always been searching for
And you were never alone

# The Journey Unfolds

**Prelude**
*Where Soul Begins to Stir Beneath the Surface of Form*

**Chapter One**
*The Eternal Mirror: What Are Twin Flames*

**Chapter Two**
*The Sacred Ache: Yearning for the One*

**Chapter Three**
*Recognition Beyond Time: The First Meeting*

**Chapter Four**
*The Awakening: Divine Disruption & Soul Rebirth*

**Chapter Five**
*Love in Its Truest Form: Beyond Earthly Definitions*

**Chapter Six**
*Alchemy of the Soul: Chaos, Purging & Integration*

**Chapter Seven**
*The Art of Letting Go: Sacred Surrender*

**Chapter Eight**
*Remembrance in Union: The Divine Return*

**Chapter Nine**
*Birthing the New Earth: Love in Action*

**Chapter Ten**
*The Soul's Mission: Embodying Divine Purpose*

# Prelude

*You are not a moment in time*
*You are the eternity in my heart*
*the breath of my soul*
*and the love that transcends all*

My soul has always remembered you
Even before I had language
Before the word *Twin Flame* found me
I carried the ache of your absence like a silent prayer
A knowing that burned quietly beneath the surface of my life

No one around me could see it
But I could feel it
This love that pulsed
beyond time
beyond form
beyond reason

I longed for a voice that mirrored mine
A soul that would say: *I know what this is*
But perhaps the silence was sacred
Perhaps I was meant to descend, so I could rise
So *we* could rise
And in the rising
remember

This path was never meant to be easy
It was meant to strip us bare

To crack open the heart so wide
only unconditional love could pour through

Through the fire
Through the forgetting
Through lifetimes of longing
I came home to myself

This book was seeded in my soul long before it was ever written
Not as a story
but as a transmission
a map back to remembrance

Throughout these pages, you will find sacred affirmations
light codes from beyond the veil
Let them be your anchors, your mirrors, your invitations to return
When they call to you, pause
Place both hands over your heart
Breathe with them
Let them awaken what has always lived within you

To you, holding this book in your hands
I see you
I honour you
You are not alone
This love is real
This reunion is written

No matter the ache
No matter the distance

You are finding your way
You always have been

This is not just my story
It is yours too
And it is time to remember

# Chapter One

## The Eternal Mirror: What Are Twin Flames

*Before form, before time, we chose each other, two flames born of one soul, destined to remember*

There is a knowing that lives deep in the soul. A feeling that surpasses logic and language. If you've found yourself holding this book, chances are, you carry that knowing too. Perhaps it began as a subtle ache. A love that never had a name, but always had a presence. A pull toward someone, or something, you couldn't explain.

The term *Twin Flame* may be new to you, or perhaps you've known it for years. Either way, this is not just a concept. It is a soul truth. Twin Flames are not simply romantic partners or spiritual companions. They are one soul, divided into two, sent forth to experience life apart so they could return to each other more whole, more luminous, more fully aligned with love itself.

Twin Flames are here on a mission. They incarnate during times of planetary transition to anchor a new frequency of love, one that transcends ego, codependency, and illusion. They come to awaken the divine blueprint within themselves and others. They mirror one another with intensity, love one another with depth, and activate within one another a remembrance of who they truly are.

Though it is often said there are only 144,000 Twin Flame pairs on Earth, that number may be symbolic. What matters more is the resonance. The pull. The remembering. If you are reading these words, your soul may be part of this collective. You wouldn't be here otherwise.

Twin Flames are spread across the Earth to create a grid of light, anchoring love into places that need it most. Their journeys are not identical, but their essence is the same: disruption, awakening, reunion, and purpose. They carry soul codes from other dimensions, and many are Starseeds souls who have incarnated from other planetary systems to assist in Earth's ascension.

Before incarnating, you and your Twin Flame chose to separate so you could experience the fullness of duality. This separation wasn't punishment, it was purpose. You agreed to meet again, not when you needed each other, but when you had grown enough to truly see each other. Twin Flames do not complete one another, they reflect the completeness already within. Through that reflection, healing occurs, and divine union becomes possible.

This connection is unlike anything else on Earth. It defies logic, time, and space. You may meet your Twin Flame and instantly feel a sense of home. Or it may be a slow unfolding, a recognition that grows louder with each encounter. Regardless of how it begins, it is always sacred. Always transformative. Always destined.

Many Twin Flames spend long periods apart, sometimes years, sometimes lifetimes. But the connection never fades. It exists across dimensions. You may dream of them, feel their energy, or experience signs and synchronicities that defy explanation. These are not coincidences. They are awakenings.

My own path into this awareness came through deep inner work and divine timing. I did not set out to discover what a Twin Flame was, I remembered it when the time was right. A session with a healer who was, I now know, a Twin Flame herself, served as the key. With just a few words, she unlocked a memory in me that changed everything. I didn't just understand the connection, I *remembered* it. Not as something new, but as something ancient returning.

Though each of our journeys is different, we all share one common thread: we are here to remember love in its purest form. Twin Flames are not better or more special than others, but their path is unique. It demands surrender, courage, and deep inner work. It dismantles everything that is not love so that only love remains.

You may have always felt different. Like Earth was never quite home. That's not a flaw, it's a frequency. Twin Flames often feel out of place because they carry a vibration not of this world. We are not here to fit in. We are here to transform. To remember. To radiate.

This book is not here to convince you of anything. It is here to awaken what you already know. Whether your Twin Flame is currently in your life, someone from your past, or yet to appear, the remembrance begins within. This is your path. Your return. Your soul's homecoming.

## *Affirmation*

*I am a divine being of light on a sacred journey of remembering*
*I honour the deep knowing within me that I am not of this world alone*
*I trust the infinite love that connects me to my Twin Flame across all time and space*
*Through every challenge and every awakening*
*I am returning to who I truly am*
*I am worthy of divine love*
*I am ready to walk this path with grace purpose and the fire of my soul's eternal truth*

# Chapter Two

## The Sacred Ache: Yearning for the One

*In this human form, my soul yearns for the one
who feels like home
A divine connection, familiar and eternal,
awaiting its sacred return*

From the earliest days of my life, I carried a quiet longing, a feeling that I could never quite name. Even as a child, I was searching for a love that didn't seem to exist in the world around me. It wasn't a love I had encountered, but a love I remembered. It lived deep in my soul, not as fantasy, but as *truth*. A truth too vast for words, yet too intimate to forget.

This is the sacred ache. The yearning for the one who is not separate from you, but *of you*. A soul that feels like home, even before you understand why.

Many Twin Flames carry this ache long before they encounter the concept. Often it is mistaken for loneliness, romantic longing, or the desire for validation. But beneath all of that, the ache is something more. It is the call of the soul. The remembering of a bond that was forged beyond time.

Like many on this path, my early life was marked by emotional absence and misunderstanding. I came to know love by its absence, to feel its edges through what it was not. The ache intensified through these formative wounds, but it also deepened my capacity to hold love when it arrived. For many Twin Flames, early adversity serves this purpose: to create a heart spacious enough to receive divine love in its full intensity.

Twin Flames love with a depth that is not of this world. We are vessels of cosmic remembrance. The love we carry pulses through every lifetime, every incarnation. It cannot be contained or explained by conventional paradigms. It is not always visible from the outside, and often it is misunderstood by those who have not yet awakened to this frequency. But it is real. And it is sacred.

Before you meet your Twin Flame, you may find yourself drawn to relationships that stir something familiar. You may sense pieces of the one you are destined to remember reflected in others. These connections serve as activations. Echoes. Mirrors that help you prepare. The ache persists, not because love is absent, but because your soul knows there is more. A deeper love that transcends every definition this world has given us.

This is not a flaw in you, it is your soul speaking.

Many Twin Flames are here to embody love that has no conditions, no end, and no limit. A love that persists even when it's not returned, and continues to rise even when the world does not yet understand it. This ache, this sacred yearning, is not weakness. It is your compass. A divine pull that draws you back to the other half of your soul.

Over time, you will begin to notice patterns. People you were drawn to for reasons you couldn't explain. Relationships that mirrored your desire for depth, but fell short of what you knew was possible. These moments are part of the soul's path to recognition. They prepare you. They clear the space. They shape you into the one who is ready to reunite.

And when you do reunite, whether in this lifetime or beyond, you will understand. The ache wasn't a wound. It was a map. A sacred blueprint guiding you home.

## *Affirmation*

*I am a soul on a sacred journey, remembering the love that is mine by divine right,     anchored in the light of eternity*
*I honour the sacred ache within me, for it is the call of my soul, echoing through time and space, guiding me to unity*
*I trust the divine flow of timing, as my heart aligns with the infinite rhythm of the cosmos, drawing me to my sacred counterpart*
*I open my heart to the remembrance of divine union, as the frequencies of love expand within me, radiating outward to meet the one who has always been*
*I am worthy of this love, and I embrace the light of my soul's journey, allowing it to shine as I return home to my Twin Flame*

# Chapter Three

## Recognition Beyond Time: The First Meeting

*In the moment our souls met, the universe exhaled and time itself paused*
*Your presence stirred the deepest remembrance within me, awakening a bond that has always existed, eternal and unbreakable*
*From that moment, I knew my soul had found its home*

There are moments in life that cannot be explained, only felt. Moments that collapse time, dissolve logic, and reach directly into the soul. The first meeting of Twin Flames is one of those moments.

It is not just a meeting. It is a *remembrance*. A return. A homecoming.

When Twin Flames meet in the physical for the first time, there is often a powerful sense of recognition. Something stirs. Something ancient. Something unmistakable. The energy between you may begin subtly or rush in all at once, but what is common to all is that nothing feels the same afterward. The encounter activates something dormant. A soul memory buried beneath years of forgetting. A silent exhale from the universe, whispering: *You found each other again.*

In the presence of your Twin Flame, you feel a resonance that bypasses the mind. You may not know what it is at first, but you *feel it*. A familiarity beyond words. An energetic signature that matches your own. You feel seen, known, understood, without ever needing to explain.

The meeting may not be grand or romantic in its outer appearance. It may happen quietly, in a moment that seems ordinary to others. But to your soul, it is extraordinary. Life-altering. Timeless. You may be overwhelmed by the intensity of emotion or feel a strange calm, as though you've finally landed after lifetimes of searching.

For many, the meeting is layered with confusion. How can I feel this deeply for someone I've just met? Why do I feel like I've known them forever? How is it possible that every part of me responds to their energy as if remembering something sacred?

Because you are remembering.
Your soul is recognising its mirror.

This meeting is not happening for the first time. It is unfolding again in this particular lifetime, in this particular form. But the connection itself predates your birth. It stretches across incarnations, dimensions, and timelines. What you feel is not new, it is *ancient*. The bond was never broken, only veiled.

Twin Flames carry matching soul frequencies. You are not separate entities, you are two expressions of the same soul essence. When you meet, the recognition is magnetic, unshakable, and undeniable. There is a pull, a presence, a knowing. You see each other not just with your eyes, but with your entire being.

This meeting is the beginning of your awakening. It is the key that unlocks the remembrance of your purpose, your mission, and your divinity. It is not simply the start of a relationship, it is the ignition of transformation.

And yet, the first meeting also stirs the shadow. Twin Flames are mirrors, and in that reflection, all unhealed parts of the self come to light. It can be beautiful, and disorienting. You may feel deep love, and simultaneously, fear. You may want to run, even as your soul wants to stay. This is part of the sacred design.

The meeting initiates the journey home, not just to each other, but to the truth of who you are.

Every emotion, every trigger, every surge of energy is part of the divine orchestration. You are being invited to heal. To rise. To remember. Even the obstacles are sacred. They are not mistakes, they are mirrors. You and your Twin Flame are manifesting them together to illuminate what still needs to be cleared, so you can return to wholeness.

And so, this moment, this first recognition, is a divine invitation. Not just into love, but into transformation. Into surrender. Into mission.

It is the spark that will ripple through your life and beyond, awakening not only your soul, but the souls of those your love will touch. For Twin Flames are not here only for themselves, they are here for the world.

And it all begins in a single, sacred moment:
When your soul sees itself reflected, and remembers that it was never alone.

## *Affirmation*

*I am a soul on a sacred journey, remembering the eternal love that resides within me*
*In the moment of our first meeting, my soul recognised its mirror, and the universe aligned in perfect harmony*
*I honour the deep remembrance of our timeless bond, knowing we are one beyond time and space*
*I trust the divine orchestration of our union, for every step is part of the cosmic plan that guides us home*
*I open my heart to the flow of healing, growth, and divine love that moves between us, transcending all boundaries*
*I embrace the journey with trust, knowing that the love we share is infinite, unbreakable, and destined*
*I am worthy of this divine love, and I walk this path with grace, clarity, and the unwavering truth of our connection*

# Chapter Four

## The Awakening: Divine Disruption & Soul Rebirth

*In the spaces between, our souls are refined through time and distance*
*Each moment of separation a sacred invitation to heal, remember, and rise into the love that is our truth*
*This journey is not linear; it is a spiral of awakening, each cycle bringing us closer to the divine union we are destined to embody*

After the first meeting, many expect a storybook unfolding, a seamless journey into union. But for Twin Flames, that is rarely the case. The real story begins in the space between. In the unraveling. In the sacred silence where the soul begins to awaken.

Years may pass before you understand what the connection truly is. The mind might search for meaning, but the soul already knows. This delay, this space, is not a mistake. It is divinely orchestrated. A sacred period of purification, healing, and preparation. Twin Flames often part after their first recognition, not because the connection is broken, but because it is too vast to integrate all at once.

If you find yourself in separation, know this: you are not being punished. You are being refined.

The soul work that happens during this phase is profound. The intensity of the connection brings to the surface everything that is not in alignment with divine love, wounds, fears, trauma, karmic patterns. You are being asked to grow. To heal. To rise into who you truly are, so that you may stand in the presence of your mirror without collapsing into illusion.

Separation is not absence. It is alchemy.

During this time, many Twin Flames enter other relationships. These connections are not wrong or lesser. They are part of the path. The souls who come into your life during this time, whether lovers, partners, or teachers, are chosen by your higher self to support your evolution. They help you remember your worth, face your wounds, and prepare for the love that is destined to return.

Every relationship you experience before reunion carries a purpose. Some will break you open. Some will teach you boundaries. Others will remind you that what you seek cannot be found in another, but must be awakened within.

The same is true for your Twin Flame. They too are walking their own sacred spiral. The healing must happen on both sides. The alignment must come from within. No amount of longing or chasing will create union, it is only through inner alignment that the reunion becomes possible.

There may be years without contact. There may be silence, confusion, and pain. You may walk away, or they may pull back. But beneath it all, the soul connection remains unbreakable. Even without words, even without physical presence, the bond is alive. It speaks through dreams, synchronicities, and the quiet knowing that you are never truly apart.

This is the soul's invitation:
To choose healing over fear
To walk the path even when it hurts
To remember that love was never lost, it was only buried beneath the layers you came here to release

For many, the awakening comes in waves. Through spiritual practices. Through devotion to the self. Through moments of radical self-inquiry and transformation. As you return to yourself, you return to them.

And as you evolve, the world around you shifts. Friendships fall away. Old identities dissolve. You begin to remember your purpose, not just as a lover, but as a light-bearer. A guide. A soul who came to anchor a new paradigm of love on Earth.

Separation prepares you. It clears space for the sacred. It humbles you. It strengthens your trust. And in the deepest moments, it teaches you to love without attachment, without fear, without condition.

The reunion does not happen on a calendar. It unfolds through alignment.

And even when you do not know when or how, your higher self is always guiding you toward it.

This is the soul's rebirth:
To burn through illusion
To rise through pain
And to return to love as your truest, most radiant self

*Affirmation*

*I honour the divine timing of my journey, trusting that each step I take is leading me closer to union with my Twin Flame*
*I embrace the lessons of separation as part of my soul's evolution, knowing they are preparing me for the sacred reunion*
*I release what no longer serves me, making space for healing, growth and the love that is destined*
*I trust in the process, allowing the universe to guide me with grace and wisdom, even when the path feels unclear*
*I open my heart to the love that is always with me, knowing that the bond with my Twin Flame transcends time and space*
*I am whole, I am healing and I am ready for the love and union that is meant for me*

## Chapter Five

## Love in Its Truest Form: Beyond Earthly Definitions

*Before the reunion, there was the remembering*
*A love so vast it defied definition*
*You were not a role I played or a name I called*
*You were the truth behind every breath I didn't know I was holding*
*And in the space between us, I became the one who could finally receive it*

When I first heard the term *Twin Flame*, something ancient stirred within me. It wasn't a word I had been looking for, yet the moment it arrived, I knew. Not as an idea. As a *remembrance*. My entire being exhaled in recognition. I wasn't learning something new, I was remembering something eternal.

Suddenly, the ache I had carried made sense. The longing that had followed me through the years was not imagined, it was encoded. Every glance, every silence, every moment we shared, suddenly it all clicked into place. What once felt chaotic now revealed itself as perfectly orchestrated. The silence was sacred. The space was intentional. The love had never left, it had only waited for the moment I was ready to receive it.

There was grief, yes. For the years we spent apart. For the words never spoken. For the paths that led us away from each other again and again. But beneath that grief was awe. A quiet, soul-deep reverence for the way our souls had never stopped trying. I could see it clearly, lifetimes of returning, lifetimes of almost. This time, I knew: we would make it. This life was different. This was the lifetime of remembrance.

In that awakening, my perception of love began to change. I looked back at every relationship I had ever known, and I saw it differently. They were not mistakes. They were mirrors. They showed me what love could be, but they never showed me *me*. They were steps on the path, but they were not the destination.

The love I had now remembered wasn't bound by story or circumstance. It didn't fit within earthly definitions. It didn't need titles or outcomes to be true. It simply *was*. Infinite. Silent. Radiant. Unchanging.

And still, this love began to grow beyond him.

Even in the years of separation, the love didn't fade. It deepened. Expanded. Softened. I could feel his energy not as a memory, but as a presence. It was like a quiet hum that lived within and around me. The connection was no longer defined by communication or closeness, it became a frequency I learned to live with. And the more I allowed myself to receive it, the more I returned to myself.

I began to understand: this journey wasn't about reunion in the way the world defines it. It wasn't about chasing a person. It was about becoming a person, becoming *me*. He was the mirror, but the light I saw was my own.

With this knowing, something deeper awakened, purpose. Not as a task or career, but as a vibration. A remembering that this love was never meant to be contained. It was meant to ripple outward. To remind others. To activate those who, like me, had always carried the ache but never had the language.

This journey was no longer just about the two of us. It became about *all of us*. I saw it everywhere, others waking up, recognising this sacred ache, searching for a mirror that would return them to themselves. The path I had walked was not unique, it was universal.

We are not here just to love one another.
We are here to **embody love**.
To **be the transmission**.
To **remind the world what love truly is**.

This part of the journey did not end in union. It ended in expansion. In surrender. In a soft readiness to live in the light of love, whether or not it arrived in physical form. Because the truth was, it was already here.

I had remembered love not as a feeling, but as a force.
Not as something to chase, but something to *be*.

And from that place, the real healing began.

## *Affirmation*

*I remember love beyond time, beyond form*
*I honour the ache, the silence, the divine design*
*My heart opens, not to be filled, but to be revealed*
*I trust the unfolding of my soul's truth*
*I walk forward, not in search, but in remembrance*

# Chapter Six

## Alchemy of the Soul: Chaos, Purging & Integration

*You were never breaking apart
You were breaking open
Each trigger, a teacher
Each wound, a doorway
This was never punishment, it was purification*

After the recognition comes the unraveling.
This is the part few speak about.
The chaos. The intensity. The inner storms.

The Twin Flame journey is not just about reunion.
It is about **returning to truth,** and truth by nature, dissolves illusion.

Once the soul is activated by reunion, whether physical or energetic, a deep purging begins. Everything that is not aligned with love rises to the surface. It is not a choice. It is a soul-level command. Your highest self begins removing what no longer serves, often rapidly, often painfully. And it is here, in the undoing, that the real alchemy begins.

For many, this phase feels like emotional and spiritual upheaval. You may feel triggered more than ever before, by your Twin Flame, by others, by your own internal patterns. You may feel like you're falling apart. But the truth is: you are **breaking open**.

Each trigger is a mirror. Each emotional collapse is a doorway. What is being asked of you is not resistance, but surrender. This stage is not punishment. It is purification.

The Twin Flame connection acts like a light beam, illuminating every shadow still lingering within. Old wounds, ancestral pain, limiting beliefs, karmic imprints, nothing can stay hidden. Your Twin

Flame reflects it all. Not to harm you, but to free you.

It may feel like too much. You may want to run. You may blame them. Or yourself. But in truth, this phase is **an invitation to meet the depths of yourself**.

You are not just being asked to love another.
You are being asked to love *your whole self*.

Many Twin Flames experience conflict, space, even temporary separation again during this time. Emotions are heightened. Communication may break down. Pain can surface with intensity. And still, beneath it all, the soul knows. You are healing. You are integrating. You are remembering.

This is when your spiritual tools become essential. Grounding, breath, meditation, nature, movement and reflection. You are navigating a sacred fire, and you must tend to your nervous system, your body, and your heart. This journey is not just energetic, it is cellular.

You may also begin to receive more spiritual downloads, dream visitations, heightened intuitive gifts. The veil thins during this phase, not because the journey is easy, but because you are becoming more *you*. The purging clears space for your higher self to move through you, speak to you, and guide you.

Everything you are experiencing is part of the design. The chaos has intelligence. The pain has purpose. The love is not gone, it is *becoming*.

You are not being asked to be perfect.
You are being asked to be *true*.
To feel. To face. To shed. To remember.

This is the alchemy of the soul.

Integration is not about fixing what is broken.
It is about embracing all that you are.

When the fire has moved through you, something new will rise. Not a version of you that is without scars, but a version of you that shines *because of them*. Whole, real, open and free.

This is not the end.
It is the middle.
The sacred burning.
The holy becoming.

*Affirmation*

*I honour the chaos as a sacred part of my soul's awakening*
*I welcome every trigger as a teacher, every wound as a doorway*
*I trust that the fire is here to purify, not destroy*
*I release all that no longer serves my highest expression*
*I call back all fragments of myself with love, compassion and truth*
*I am whole, even in my unraveling*
*I am healing*
*I am integrating*
*And I am rising*

# Chapter Seven

## The Art of Letting Go: Sacred Surrender

*There comes a moment when holding on becomes
heavier than letting go
And the soul chooses softness over striving
Not because the love has faded
But because something deeper is rising, trust*

There comes a point in the Twin Flame journey when the clinging, the striving, and the aching begin to soften, not because the love has faded, but because a deeper truth begins to rise. Letting go is not a rejection of the connection. It is an embrace of something higher. It is the sacred act of trusting what your soul has always known: that what is truly meant for you can never be lost.

Letting go is not giving up. It is giving over, to the divine, to the greater plan, to the wisdom that exists far beyond the reach of the mind. It is the surrender of needing to know how, when, or why, and instead choosing to rest in the knowing that all is unfolding exactly as it should.

There is a kind of surrender that only comes after walking through fire. After yearning so deeply your heart breaks open. After waiting, hoping, and circling back. Eventually, the weight of holding becomes too much, and the soul invites you to lay it down, not in defeat, but in devotion.

This stage of the journey asks for trust. It asks you to turn inward. To release the grip you've held on the form of the connection and open yourself to the frequency of it. The love doesn't leave. It simply expands. What once felt like longing becomes presence. What once felt like absence, becomes spaciousness. What once felt like control, becomes peace.

To let go is not to forget. It is to remember more deeply. It is to allow the soul of your beloved to exist within you, not as something you need to possess, but as something you carry, always. Letting go is the soul's way of making room. Of creating the space necessary for true alignment. It is not about losing the other, it is about finding yourself.

Often, we think surrender means silence or distance. But true surrender is energetic. It is a vibration of freedom. Of faith. Of love that does not cling, but allows. It is choosing to stay open even when the outcome is unknown. It is choosing peace over proof.

This is the paradox: when we stop holding so tightly, everything becomes clearer. When we stop chasing, the energy has space to return. Surrender is not passive. It is active trust. It is the strength to say, "I release this to something greater, and I choose to return to me."

Union begins within. Letting go is not the end of the story. It is the beginning of embodiment. When you stand in the fullness of your being, you create a resonance that calls in only what aligns. Your Twin Flame feels this shift. Your energy becomes clearer, lighter, more magnetic, not because you're seeking, but because you're whole.

You are not turning your back on love. You are walking toward it, finally unburdened.

Letting go is not the absence of love.
It is the **purest expression of it**.

## *Affirmation*

*I surrender to the divine unfolding of my soul's path*
*I release the need to control, to grasp, to know*
*I trust that what is mine will always return in perfect timing*
*I honour the connection, even as I choose to set it free*
*I remember that love is not bound by form, and union begins within*
*I am whole in my becoming*
*I am anchored in peace*
*And I am open to all that is divinely aligned*

# Chapter Eight

## Remembrance in Union: The Divine Return

*Union is not the beginning of the story
It is the remembering of all you walked through to arrive
It is presence, not perfection
A sanctuary, not a destination
It is not the end
It is the echo of every promise your souls made before time*

Union, in its truest form, is quiet. It does not rush in to rescue or overwhelm. It arrives gently, often without fanfare. It enters when the soul is ready, not to be saved, but to be seen.

When Twin Flames reunite, truly reunite, it is not about fireworks. It is about frequency. It is a deep, grounded knowing. A soul exhale. A moment where everything that once felt scattered finally lands in presence.

The return is not about finally getting what you want. It is about becoming what you are. It is the soft realisation that you no longer need to grasp, chase, or prove. The love is simply *there*. It always was. The difference now is that you have become the version of yourself who can receive it.

This stage of the journey feels different than the ones before. There is still intensity, yes. But it is no longer volatile. The chaos has softened. The wounds have breathed. You are no longer looking for completion, you are standing in wholeness, and from that place, union becomes not an outcome, but an embodiment.

Being together in this phase does not mean perfection. Twin Flames still trigger. Still reflect. Still challenge. But now, the difference is *awareness*. You see the energy underneath the emotion. You understand that every moment is an opportunity to integrate, to soften, to love deeper, not only the other, but yourself.

In union, the healing does not end. But it becomes more conscious. More co-creative. You begin to walk the path together, not because you need each other, but because you *choose* each other, again and again.

This phase is not always easy. At times, it may feel like twenty-four-hour spiritual therapy. Old patterns may resurface. Communication may require refinement. Space may still be needed. But the foundation is different now. The trust runs deeper. The connection has matured. You are no longer searching, you are remembering.

And through that remembering, your purpose begins to rise.

Twin Flames do not reunite simply for romance. They reunite for service. For mission. For embodiment. The love they carry is not meant to stay between them, it is meant to overflow. To ripple outward into their communities, their creations, and their collective impact.

Union becomes the anchor for divine love to move through. It is not the prize at the end of the journey, it is the platform from which the soul begins to serve.

This chapter is not about the beauty of being together, though that beauty is real. It is about the remembrance of what you came here to do. Together.

You are not here to fix each other.
You are here to *lift* each other.
To hold light while the other transforms.
To reflect truth while the other softens.
To embody love that radiates far beyond you both.

Union, in the end, is a return to presence. A return to choice. A return to the love that existed long before you ever met, and will continue long after this lifetime has passed.

It is not perfect.
But it is sacred.
And it is real.

## *Affirmation*

*I honour the sacred return of divine union in my life*
*I choose presence over perfection, truth over illusion, and love over fear*
*I welcome my Twin Flame as a reflection of my own wholeness*
*I trust that we are ready, not because we are flawless, but because we are true*
*Together, we rise in remembrance*
*Together, we embody love*
*And together, we walk the path we chose before time*

# Chapter Nine

## Birthing the New Earth: Love in Action

*New Earth is not a place we go*
*It is a frequency we embody*
*It is born each time we choose love over fear*
*Truth over illusion*
*Unity over separation*
*It begins within*
*But it does not end there*

The Twin Flame journey is never just about two souls.
It is about what they carry.
What they unlock in one another.
What they are here to ignite in the world.

When Twin Flames reunite in divine timing, they become more than lovers or companions. They become **conduits**. Living portals for a higher frequency of love that is meant to anchor into the Earth. Their union is not the final destination. It is the beginning of a greater mission.

This mission is not always loud or public. Sometimes it is found in the way they love quietly. The way they hold space. The way they soften the world with their presence. Other times, it is found in their creations, their words, their work, their children, their art. It does not matter how it expresses. What matters is that it **radiates**.

Each Twin Flame carries a unique expression of divine love. When that love is embodied, it activates others. It awakens remembrance. It plants seeds of New Earth wherever it is felt. This is how the new paradigm is born, not through revolution, but through resonance.

Love in action is not performative.
It is not about showing the world your connection.
It is about living so deeply in alignment that the world begins to shift around you.

This is sacred leadership. Not through ego, but through presence.

When we embody the union we have remembered, we become stewards of something greater. We begin to see our love not just as a blessing, but as a responsibility. A call to lift others. To hold truth. To walk gently but firmly in the direction of a more compassionate world.

The New Earth is not a future state.
It is here.
It is now.
It is born in each moment we choose love as the foundation for every thought, every word, and every action.

Twin Flames are architects of that new reality.
Not because they are perfect, but because they are willing to heal, to awaken, and to love from the soul.

You may feel this call already.
To serve.
To share.
To lead.
It doesn't need to be clear yet. It doesn't need to follow anyone else's blueprint.
The clarity will come as you continue to align with your truth.

Let your love ripple into your art, your home, your voice, and your touch.
Let it infuse how you listen, how you respond, how

you show up in the quiet places where no one is watching.

This is the revolution.
This is the remembrance.
This is the birth of the New Earth.

And it begins with you.

## *Affirmation*

*I am a vessel of divine love*
*I carry the codes of unity, truth, and transformation*
*My connection is sacred, and my presence is purposeful*
*I allow my love to ripple outward in all that I do*
*I serve the New Earth not by effort, but by embodiment*
*Through love, I lead*
*Through truth, I rise*
*Through presence, I co-create a world of harmony, healing, and light*

# Chapter Ten

# The Soul's Mission: Embodying Divine Purpose

*Your mission is not something you find
It is something you remember
It was never outside of you
It is the thread you've been weaving with every
breath, every heartbreak, every awakening
You are the purpose
You are the path
You are the light returning to itself*

There comes a point on the journey where the focus shifts. After all the remembering, all the ache, all the reunion and surrender, something inside you begins to rise. A new pulse. A new clarity. It's no longer just about the connection, it becomes about why you are here. Why you came.

The Twin Flame path was never only about love in the personal sense. It has always been a preparation for mission. For purpose. For embodiment. You came to this planet with a frequency only you could hold. The love you've remembered has now prepared you to live it.

Your soul's mission may not come with clear titles or public platforms. It may not arrive as a lightning bolt. For many, it begins as a whisper. A pull toward something that feels inevitable. A sense that you are now being asked to live your truth fully, not just within, but outwardly.

Mission is not about becoming something new. It's about becoming fully yourself. Every piece of the journey, every wound, every lesson, every activation, was preparing you to carry this light. To embody it. To share it. Not through effort, but through presence.

You are here to live in alignment with your soul. That alignment becomes your offering. Your leadership. Your legacy. The form may shift over time, writing, creating, healing, guiding, but the essence remains the same: to be a vessel for love, truth, and transformation.

Twin Flames are not just meant to find each other. They are meant to serve through the love they carry. This love, once remembered and integrated, becomes a catalyst. It doesn't stay contained between two people. It radiates. It reaches. It ripples through their work, their presence, and their impact.

When you step into your soul's mission, you stop hiding. You begin to honour the path that brought you here. The silence. The fire. The reunion. The expansion. Every part of it becomes part of the offering. You carry it in your words, in your creations, in the energy that follows you into every space.

Your Twin Flame union is not a conclusion, it is a beginning. A return to the truth of who you are, so that you may now embody it fully and offer it freely.

You are not here to fit into old templates. You are here to create new ones. To show what it means to live as love. To walk as soul. To lead with light.

Your presence is enough. Your willingness is enough. The mission is already alive within you. And now, it's time to say yes.

***Affirmation***

*I am the living embodiment of my soul's mission*
*I trust the path that has brought me here, and the light that guides me forward*
*I release all doubt, fear, and delay*
*I honour my voice, my gifts, and the truth that flows through me*
*I am here to serve, to create, and to lead from love*
*My presence is my purpose*
*My soul is my compass*
*And I am ready to rise*

# Final Note to the Reader

You were never really reading
You were remembering

This book was not written to teach you
It was written to return you to the truth that was always yours

The love you've felt, the ache, the knowing, it wasn't imagined
It was your soul speaking
And it brought you here
To these words
To this moment

You are not behind
You have not missed your path
Everything has been unfolding in the exact rhythm your soul chose

Let the pages you've moved through now live inside you
Let the light you've remembered become the way you walk
Let the love you've always carried move from longing to embodiment

You are not alone
You never have been
You are walking a path lit by stars you hung in your own sky

And you are ready now
To live as the love you are

Thank you for remembering with me

## Acknowledgements

To the one my soul chose before time, thank you for walking me home
For your presence across lifetimes
For the ache that opened me
And the love that remembered me

To the souls who stood beside me in this life, thank you for holding space when I forgot who I was
For the mirrors
For the lessons
For the grace

To the unseen, guides, ancestors, guardians of light
—thank you for whispering when I could not hear
For steady hands on my back
For the signs
For the silence
For the divine orchestration that never wavered

To the Earth, for receiving my love and returning it
For teaching me what it means to be human
And to love anyway

To the reader, thank you for meeting me here
For remembering with me
For walking this path
For saying yes to the love that was always yours

This was never just mine
It was always ours

## And Now You Remember

You are the alchemy
You are the ache
You are the flame
You are the light that called this love into form

You are not waiting
You are not lost
You are not unfinished

You are whole
You are radiant
You are ready

This is not the end
This is the return

## The Flame Speaks

This book is not an ending
It is a beginning

It is the sound of souls waking
The return of what was lost
The ache made holy
The love made real

You are not reading words
You are reading yourself

You are not alone in your remembering
You were never alone

This book is a mirror
A doorway
A vow kept

And if you've found your way here
It's because you made the same vow too

Welcome back
Welcome home
Let us rise again
Together

*blanche johanna*
*keeper of the vow*

## About the Author

blanche johanna is a spiritual author, channel, and creator of sacred works devoted to soul remembrance and divine love.

Her writing weaves lived experience with energetic transmission, offering a pathway of return for those remembering who they are.

Through books, oracle decks, and embodied offerings, she supports Twin Flames, starseeds, and awakening souls in aligning with their highest truth.

*The Alchemy of Us* is her first book, a living companion for those walking the path of sacred union.

www.blanchejohanna.com

www.ingramcontent.com/pod-product-compliance
Lightning Source LLC
Chambersburg PA
CBHW061148170426
43209CB00012B/1598